JAYVON'S ADVENTUROUS WALK

by Sanjerettia Hughes

Jayvon laid in the grass.

Jayvon went on his evening walk.

Jayvon spent time with his friends hanging out!

Jayvon had fun with his friends.
He decided to head home.

Jayvon thought, "I can go to the beach on the way home!"

"hi there!"
"hello"

Jayvon went to the park!
The kids really liked Jayvon.

Jayvon was really happy to play in the green grass.

Jayvon saw a dancing pig, he thought that was so funny. He laughed so hard, that he started to cry!

Jayvon had an adventurous day. It was time to get home from his long walk.

Jayvon could see his house from afar.

Jayvon was finally back at home.

Jayvon's Adventurous Walk

Thanks for supporting me in purchasing this book

This book is dedicated to my
first grandson Jayvon

www.ingramcontent.com/pod-product-compliance
Lightning Source LLC
LaVergne TN
LVHW071113160826
845679LV00004B/1058

9798367959215